Lifestyle Coach Doctors

Susan Kersley

While every precaution has been taken in the preparation of this book, the publisher assumes no responsibility for errors or omissions, or for damages resulting from the use of the information contained herein.

LIFESTYLE COACHING FOR DOCTORS

Table of Contents

PREFACE 6

PART ONE - WHAT IS COACHING? 7

1.WHAT IS COACHING? 8

2.WHAT CAN COACHING DO FOR YOU? 9

3.SKILLS TAUGHT BY LIFE COACHES. 11

4.THE ROLES A COACH CAN PLAY 13

5.WHAT EXACTLY DOES A COACH DO? 15

6. WHY FEEDBACK IS IMPORTANT 17

7. COACHING FOR SUPPORT 18

8. WORKING WITH A COACH 20

PART TWO – COACHING + DOCTORS 22

9. FIND YOUR PERFECT BALANCE 23

10. SUCCESSFUL COACHING 24

11. COACHING BY AND FOR DOCTORS 26

12.DOES COACHING BENEFIT DOCTORS? 30

13. WHAT DOCTORS NEED TO KNOW 33

14. MYTHS ABOUT COACHING 35

PART THREE- COACHING DOCTORS....................................38

15. A WORTHWHILE NICHE? 39

16. CAN COACHING HELP DOCTORS? 45

17. WHAT DOES A COACH DO FOR DOCTORS? 49

18. DOCTORS' CHALLENGES 52

19. COACHING, ONE TO ONE OR IN A GROUP 56

20. DOCTORS KNOW ABOUT COACHING....................................59

21. 'CULTURE' OF THE MEDICAL PROFESSION 61

22. IMPROVING WORK-LIFE BALANCE?....................................63

23.TELEPHONE COACHING....................................68

PART FOUR - MY STORY....................................75

24. MY STORY....................................76

25. HOW I FOUND DOCTORS TO COACH 81

DON'T MISS OUT! 83

ALSO BY SUSAN KERSLEY 85

ABOUT THE AUTHOR 87

Preface

I wrote this book for doctors who wonder what coaching is and are considering hiring a coach. Coaching techniques help doctors when dealing with patients, and also for them to make life changes. It enables them to move forward in their decision-making. They receive non-judgmental support from the coach, someone not directly involved in their day-to-day life, yet with similar life experiences.

I was a life coach for doctors for fifteen years after I retired from medicine. I share some of my experiences of coaching doctors with you in this book.

This book is also for coaches who want to work with doctors as clients.

PART ONE - WHAT IS COACHING?

1.What is Coaching?

Coaching is a tool for increasing success and satisfaction in your life.

A coach listens, reflects and encourages you to set and reach your goals by helping you focus on achieving specific actions towards what you want.

Coaching is a forward-looking, active process, whereas counselling deals with and explores emotional issues from the past, and helps you to cope with crises.
Coaching is about improving the quality of life and creating what you want for the future. It closes the gap between how life is and how you would like it to be. It encompasses whatever areas of life or career you want it to.

With coaching, you look after your physical and emotional needs. It encourages you to have balance in all areas of your life.

You learn to say 'no' more often and set clearer boundaries, both physical and emotional. By getting rid of whatever drains your energy and increasing the things that give you more get-up-and-go, life as a doctor can improve.

2.What can Coaching do for you?

Coaching helps you to:

- **Focus on what you want.** It's important to set clear goals. It's easy to say 'I don't want such-and-such anymore.' That isn't a goal.
- **Specify what you want** instead of what you don't want.
- **Save time and effort.** Coaching offers tools and suggestions for making changes quickly so that something you've been struggling with for ages can suddenly seem easy.
- **Think about time** scale for desired outcomes, instead of waiting (for example 'when the children have left home' or 'when I've lost the weight'). Then you realise the obstacles you thought were there disappear.

Coaching:

- **Changes the way you think** about a situation. When you 'disassociate', you see a different perspective on the circumstances. This technique alone can transform your perception of a situation.
- **Clarifies what can and can't change.** When you challenge yourself, you realise you can change more than you thought.
- **Motivates you to start**. When you set goals and project your thoughts to the future, you do more than you thought possible.

- **Encourages you to say 'no' more often.** It's easier to find time to do things for yourself when you have a choice about what you do.
- **Improves your time management.** If you believe you have too much to do to make the changes you want, you set different boundaries and manage your time more effectively.
- **Focuses on your needs.** As you learn more about personal development, you realise that self-care is vital.
- **Encourages you to look after yourself.** People who care for others, whether in their work or home, are often not addressing their own needs.
- **Perfects your organisational skills**. When you clear your clutter and get more organised, other changes happen more easily
- Reduces your stress. You learn ways to communicate more effectively, to relax, and deal with stress.

3.Skills taught by life coaches

You may wonder what skills you learn by working with a life coach.

Setting goals which are specific, measurable, achievable, realistic and timed because when you know what you want, you are more likely to achieve.

Achieving goals by removing any obstacles and getting support to do that and moving forward step-by-step.

Gaining confidence and being more assertive, saying no more often, asking for help when you need it and doing what you really want to do.

Enables you to you set good boundaries. Looking at your beliefs and how they affect your life, stop you from doing certain things and realising you can change them.

Aligning life with your values so that what you do is congruent with what's important for you. When you do that, your life flows more easily. You find it becomes a pleasure to do whatever is necessary to achieve your goals.

Becoming clear about your identity, because of who you are, relates to what's important in your life.

Finding out what you want from life, and how you can work towards achieving it.

Living a healthy balanced life by treating your body well, keeping it well exercised and nourished with healthy and energising foods. When you do this, you achieve more than you ever believed possible.

Improve your relationships by better communication skills. Become familiar with rapport, and understand a situation from another person's point of view. Then you will be able to work out a way to achieve a win-win solution to a problem.

Living the life you truly want is the most important skill you learn from a coach. Too many people live their life dictated to them by their parents or their teachers. They forget that it's important to work out exactly what they want for you life rather than fulfilling the expectations of other people.

4.The roles a coach can play

You may not be aware of the roles that a coach will play in your life until you decide to hire one and experience for yourself. When you think about these roles, you will be clearer about the support yfrom working with a coach.

Mentor. You might choose a coach because you realise that he or she has been through some similar experiences, such as similar profession or life transition to your own and so will better understand your personal situation.

Non-judgmental listener. If you want someone who will listen without criticism, a coach will do just that. When you tell your story, you receive feedback without judgment.

Sounding board. It is very useful to know you can talk about ideas, without committing yourself too soon, by discussing them with a coach. As you tell someone about your possible course of action, speaking your ideas out loud helps you decide the best way forward.

Challenger. A coach gets you to think by asking challenging questions. He or she may ask you to tell them aspects of your plan that you hadn't thought about before and you become clearer about your alternative course of action.

Motivator. When you decide what you are going to do, it is useful to have a coach to encourage you to take the first steps and do what you want. Having someone to report back to about your progress is very motivating.

Enabler. The coach has experience, so may suggest what to do next. Of course, you don't have to follow those suggestions, but hearing about them may bring into your mind other ways to proceed.

Confidante. Talk in confidence to someone not directly involved in your life.

Advisor. Coaches don't give advice. However, they may share ways that worked for them in similar circumstances, so you can decide what to do.

5.What exactly does a coach do?

You may not have got around to hiring a coach because of being unclear about what a Life Coach actually does when they work with you.

A coach offers:
Listening without judgment. If you are reluctant to talk because of expected recrimination about what you are talking about, it is useful that the coach is non-judgmental.

An opportunity to brainstorm solutions to your dilemma or problem. When you talk to a coach, you discover the most appropriate way forward for you to make progress.

Questions to make you think more deeply. When you want to decide between different options, it is very useful to be challenged by questions the coach asks you. These will enable you to think about ways to proceed that you may not have considered before.

Ways to move forward. Having someone 'on your side' is very motivating and gets you to take actions you may have been procrastinating about.

Encouragement and help to get things done. Having someone who has 'been there, done that' is useful for practical pointers to take you to your next step.

A chance to talk in confidence. Just knowing you can talk without what you say going further is very useful. The coach supports your agenda.

Insight into some of their experience. Despite sharing, they don't expect you to do the same as they did, though it can be helpful for you to hear how someone else coped with something similar. Learn from what happened to them, though at the same time realise that the way each person deals with a particular circumstance may depend on their own perception and personality. However, just knowing that there might be some connection between their life and yours can be helpful.

6. Why feedback is important

The coach appreciates hearing from the client about how the coaching is helping them.

The coach asks challenging questions. The client learns how their beliefs stop them from making the progress that they want. The client gives feedback to the coach, 'It was really helpful when you asked me to think about that situation,' or 'I don't want to discuss that.' With no feedback, the coach may persist in asking the client to think about a situation not directly related to the area around which they wanted coaching.

Feedback is important from the coach to the client. For example, when working with a client on the telephone, the coach may notice something upsets the client. If the coach says 'this is something which really upsets you,' the client may connect this to their inability to achieve. Feedback to the coach is useful at the end of each session and after a period of coaching.

It's useful for the coach to ask the client about what had the most impact on them, what they would like done differently, and what message they're taking away from the session. Coaching is not only the one-to-one session, it's about the process which happens when the client thinks more deeply about what isn't working and what to do for the future.

7. Coaching for support

Part of looking after yourself is about finding the right person to support you through some tough decisions. Contacting a coach can be an enormous leap out of your comfort zone. Are you admitting not being able to find the way forward for yourself? Not at all. Contacting a coach is about recognising what you need and being aware of how to get things done at last, even those you've been dithering about for so long.

Can we ever know what is the right decision?
Perhaps you haven't committed to coaching because you want to be sure it will be the right decision.

Unless you try the things you really want to do, how can you ever know whether it's will be right or wrong for you? The value of working with a coach is unquantifiable: within a few months you will make enormous leaps in what you think, do and believe about yourself.

This is what a recent client (consultant physician) emailed me after a few weeks of coaching: *While at first, phone calls and e-mails seemed a funny way to discuss such personal matters, it really works. When I feel in danger of becoming a 'I hate my job' bore with my friends -I can tell you instead. Somehow you help me lift my head up above the endless cycle of asking myself the same questions repeatedly, and help me take control over my decisions. I think that you have helped me to gain a lot of confidence in myself over the last few months, and have helped me to do my work a lot better. While ultimately the decision is mine, it is lovely to have your support and encouragement. It is important to me you are independent with no 'angle' on my decision, unlike my husband and parents (who would prefer me to continue in my work but are coming round to the idea that they would like me to be happy.)*

The hardest thing that you have started is to help me face up to uncertainty about the future. Well, if my boss seems happy to do that - he seems confident that he could fill my job, then I should be. I find his confidence in his ability to replace me a little unnerving!

Sometimes you realise that something has to change in your life: a coach can be the catalyst you need. Many people say they want to change their lives. They take no action, so their lives stay the same and they get more and more frustrated as the years go by. Perhaps you know what you want and are ready to take action. That is wonderful because when you decide to change your life and take the first tentative step, then something magical happens. It's as if the world itself changes too. People and places seem different from the way they were before and it becomes easier to believe that what you hope for might   be   possible.

8. Working with a coach

During a time of life-change, it's motivating and useful to have a mentor or coach, someone to support you during the time of transition.

Working with a mentor or a coach is a good way to reduce overwhelm and procrastination felt by many people when they decide to change their lives.

A powerful way to move an idea forward is by using metaphor to compare something with similar attributes to the subject you are considering. For example, thinking about the changing seasons of the year is useful in relation to how you feel about aspects of your life and may help you understand how the process of change happens internally.

If you are considering leaving something, you may feel like Autumn moving towards Winter. Then you may experience a time when outwardly things are dormant and you lack energy and drive. However, inwardly things are happening. When your Spring arrives you have more energy, new hope. It is a period of growth and anticipation. Suddenly, it seems, ideas and energy fill you. You are ready to take the first steps for change. Finally, you move into Summer and your life is in full bloom again.

Working with a coach is like having someone sitting beside you for part of your life's journey. It may only be for a few sessions, or maybe for much longer.

However, once you know the road you are on and learn to navigate yourself, then you carry on and say goodbye to the coach.

PART TWO – COACHING + DOCTORS

9. Find your perfect balance

Working with a coach enables you to have a life and find your perfect balance between medicine and life.

A coach:

Pushes your buttons: so that you understand the importance of about making changes.

Encourages you to do things you hadn't considered before: so other things in your life change too.

Reminds you to keep on track with your projects so that you achieve what you want.

Follows up your promises of taking action: so you move forward.

Energises you to start: so,

that you believe in your ability to succeed.

Coaches you to find the solutions right for you: they empower you.

Talks about the pros and cons of what you might do: so you move forward with conviction.

Believes in you and your capabilities, so your self-esteem improves.

Answers your questions: so, you understand more about the process.

Listens to you fully so you respect yourself.

Alerts you to challenges: so they prepare you for them.

Never criticises your ideas: so, you feel valued.

Communicates with you appropriately so they listen to you.

Encourages you at every step: so you keep going until you achieve what you want.

10. Successful coaching

For a positive experience and outcome from coaching, you need to:

Find a suitable coach. For successful coaching, it's important to find somebody that you feel comfortable talking to about whatever challenges you have in your life. Coaching is about helping you make the decision that is right in your life. It's important that you find somebody who listens to what you say and feeds back what they hear from you, is non-judgmental about you and your life and the goals that you wish to achieve.

Decide where the coaching will take place. Successful coaching needs a place where you feel safe to talk about whatever you wish to discuss. It's best if it is a quiet room, whether you meet your coach face-to-face, on the telephone or online.

Commit to engaging with the coaching process. The success of the coaching process depends on your making changes. You must enter it with the right mindset. This means being prepared to look at how you deal with situations in a new way and prepare to try different ways to respond. It's inappropriate to start a coaching relationship if you are depressed or unable to commit to time to think about the issues you discuss during your coaching discussions.

The coach may end the coaching if other things going on in your life distract you and you do not make adjustments to allow for these.

Examine all areas of your life. Work with a coach is about achieving a specific goal. However, it is beneficial to examine how achieving affects other areas of your life and other people, too. Connected and related to the success of the coaching will be the way you look after yourself in relation to exercise, food and creative interests.

Have the confidence to move forward after coaching ends. Coaching is useful throughout your life. It enables you to move on and achieve many things that you thought you never could. Nevertheless, for many people, the coaching relationship is quite short and focused on achieving a specific goal. You will discover ways to deal with specific challenges. Once coaching has completed, you will have the confidence to deal with those challenges when they occur again.

Coaches offer you tools and tricks to make it possible for you to find the answer for yourself.

Coaching is not prescriptive: following their challenging questions, you will gain insights into your situation and find the way forward.

11. Coaching by and for doctors

Many doctors don't know that coaching enables them to achieve, or how quickly it can make a difference.

Coaching is for successful people like you, who feel something is missing.

Coaching helps doctors who don't look after themselves. They may drink excessive alcohol or start to self-medicate instead of seeking the help and support they need. As a result, these doctors may prescribe the incorrect treatment, with serious effects both for the patient and themselves.

Coaching offers support, discussion, encouragement and motivation, enabling a doctor to deal better with difficult situations with colleagues or patients and the stresses of being a doctor. When they are fit emotionally and physically, not only them but also their patients benefit.

Coaching empowers and motivates doctors to do what they want. When they recognise and satisfy their own needs, they become better at what they do.

Coaching provides them with the chance to re-think what they value in life.

Whether it's worrying about how they dealt with the last patient, preparing for a presentation for their colleagues, or trying to keep up to date with medical journal reading, a doctor's life can be very stressful.

Doctors' responsibilities are immense and the consequence of making a mistake, enormous. However, with the pressures on doctors, there is a tendency to work hard and forget how important it is to improve their work-life balance and do things apart from work.

Coaching helps doctors bring more fun and laughter into their lives and realise this is vital for their health and well-being.

A doctor is a person too. Fulfilling their needs is vital if they want to be content and happy. Some doctors think that they have to deal with challenges on their own, and that working with a coach is a sign of failure.

Quite the reverse, doctors who decide to hire a coach discover how quickly they can turn things around.

A doctor commits to doing the best for their patients; this means that they may neglect the rest of life. For a balanced life, their non-work responsibilities are also important. With a happy home life and time to do something apart from medicine, they are a better doctor with an improved work life balance.
The most common lifestyle issues that challenge doctors are:

- **lack of work-life balance**
- **ineffective time management**
- **absence of self-care**
- **lack of confidence and/or low self-esteem**

Coaching is useful because doctors are highly intelligent, self-motivated and self-sufficient, yet might be wary about talking with someone about their challenges.

Sometimes they feel stuck, yet they seem unable to take actions to get the results they want, even when they know precisely what they need to do. Then they find that coaching helps.

The challenges could be in relation to career progression, especially when there are conflicts with personal relationships and family pressures and might be, for example, about getting on further in the profession or neglecting family commitments.

Coaching can be very useful in these circumstances because:

- **It enables them to gain clarity about their situation**. They discuss details with their coach and realise what to do.
- **It is easy to talk to their coach** about their challenges. Although they may never meet face to face because they connect by telephone or online for coaching,

- **Coaching enables them to find their own solution** to a challenge or problem. Since it is not prescriptive, they discover within themself options for progress they may not have thought of previously, or dismissed as something they couldn't do.
- **Coaching encourages them to do what they want** to do and discover for themself the right way forward.
- **Coaching isn't judgmental,** unlike friends or family who may disapprove a solution.
- **Coaching is forward looking and is effective quickly**, unlike long-term counselling or therapy.
- **Energy and motivation to change** and make a difference happen within a few sessions.
- **Travel to your coaching sessions unnecessary,** as they connect on the telephone or online.
- The effectiveness of coaching is the lack of distraction from physical appearance or body language, although it may seem strange not to meet face to face.

12.Does coaching benefit doctors?

Are you a doctor wary of coaching or mentoring because you think you have to cope with challenges yourself without support?

There is something powerful about having someone to talk to, regularly, onto whom you can offload and bounce ideas, receive unconditional positive support and encouragement.

Coaching is a process that enables you to find fulfillment in your personal and professional life.

Coaching is a useful tool to increase your commitment and motivation for change.

Your coach listens. You choose the focus for the session and your coach asks challenging questions. that enable you to look at your situation and your future and decide what you need to do to take you into that desired future.

As a doctor, you may wonder if coaching might be useful for you. Something has held you back from exploring the option of hiring a coach, or becoming a coach yourself. Perhaps you thought it might be a bit 'wishy-washy' or too 'touchy-feely'.

You question if doctors can benefit from coaching since it's about finding their own solutions. Do you believe you should sort things out for yourself without involving someone who doesn't know you and who you might never meet?

If this sounds familiar, then here are some questions to ask yourself. Your answers may make it easier for you to decide if coaching would be useful.

Do you really want a different life?
A doctor's life can engulf you, so you neglect other important parts of life. Does the thought of changing seem scary so you would rather stick with what you are familiar, even if you aren't happy?

Are you prepared to talk about what isn't working for you, and picture the sort of life you would really like and discuss the options? Until you look at your future and explore possibilities, it will be difficult to make the changes you want.

Do you realise that success can include all aspects of your life, not only medicine? Many doctors define themselves in relation to their work and so strive to get to the top of their specialty and yet have an unfulfilling personal life.

Are you willing to see things from a new perspective? Remember that if you continue doing everything in the same way, then nothing changes. Even if you think the system, rather than you, has to change, there are things you can do to make this happen. This may mean expressing your concerns and telling others you are going to do something different.

Do you understand it is important to look at your whole life? That involves your partner, friends, family and community, and includes those parts of you not involved in medicine: your hobbies and outside interests and the way you look after your own health and well-being.

If 'yes' is your answer to all these questions, then read on to discover more about coaching and how it could be useful for you.

13. What doctors need to know

What are the most important things you need to know in order to benefit from coaching?

You have a choice. As a doctor you get into the habit of doing whatever they ask you to do, because you are as helpful and obliging to your patients as you can. You find it difficult to set reasonable boundaries in place around your work-related tasks. However, you have far more choice than you realise because a lot of the things that you spend your day doing are those tasks that you were told you must do when you started your job. As you get used to this setup, you may find that some of those things are unnecessary, perhaps because of improved technology. Tell the people you work with what you will or won't put up with any more.

Become more confident. Say no, and be assertive enough to develop techniques for ending a consultation when you have discussed as much as you need with the patient and it's time to move on to the next patient.

Confidence and assertiveness go together hand in hand. When you become better at these skills, you organise your day more efficiently so you finish on time. Decide when you are going to stop the work you're doing that day, and leave the hospital, or general practice surgery in order to get home at a reasonable time each day.

You can become more assertive when you state clearly to the other person what you will do or no longer do. You will also be able to tell the other people with whom you work, what you want from them, and how you want them to work differently.

Sometimes you have to use the 'stuck record technique,' in which you keep repeating your request without embellishment.

If they frequently interrupt you, without an obvious reason, then each time someone comes into your room say 'please don't disturb me until I finished with this patient.'

14. Myths about coaching

There are some myths which might concern doctors thinking of hiring a coach.

Coaching is very expensive. You use coaching to discover a solution to a problem or work out how to face up to a challenge in your life, not the time you speak to the coach and for the coach's expertise and experience. Sometimes a question from a coach will be a revelation and you realise what you must do. With coaching, you change your view of a situation and find there are solutions you hadn't thought of before.

A question from a coach is an 'aha' moment for you and you will realise what you must do.

If you have a problem and you have tried every solution you can think of and you are at your wit's end, what would you give to get that issue sorted out? You change your view of a situation when you have coaching and discover solutions you hadn't previously thought of before. How valuable is that for you?

Coaching is long term. Many people find a few sessions are effective in sorting out their challenge in a particular area. Sometimes just one session is all it takes. However, after sorting out one area of life, talk about some other aspect of your life.

Coaches tell you what to do. A good coach won't tell you what to do because coaching is about helping you find your own solutions. Coaches may interpret what they hear you say or even make some suggestions, but ultimately you decide, after reflecting on the conversation, the best way forward.

Coaching is another word for therapy. Coaching differs from counselling or psychotherapy, and there are obvious differences. Coaching is for people who have the desire and the energy to make changes and to look at their lives with a new perspective, starting from where they are today and looking forward to what they want to achieve.

Coaching is solution focussed and works well with people who are motivated and willing to try different approaches. Therapy or counseling is more suitable for people who want to understand or come to terms with their past, or those reacting to sudden traumatic changes such as bereavement or relationship break-up when they need crisis management.

Coaching is not for doctors. Coaching can enable anyone, including doctors. If you feel stuck and find it difficult to do what you want to do, a coach helps you to sort things out and take on your challenges.

Working with a coach is like having someone sitting beside you for part of your life's journey.

However, once you learn to navigate for yourself, then you carry on and say goodbye to the coach.

Coaches don't understand a doctor's life. If a vital part of coaching is that your coach understands your medical lifestyle, then choose a coach who is or was a doctor.

Coaching encourages you to take action and achieve what you want quickly.

PART THREE- COACHING DOCTORS

15. A worthwhile niche?

I started coaching doctors many years ago, after retiring early from the medical profession. I had experience in counselling and personal development, so after training in coaching and NLP (neurolinguistic programming), I set up my business.

As a doctor, I used to enjoy communicating one to one with patients, so I wanted to continue working similarly. I realised that after thirty years of working as a doctor and married to a surgeon, I had valuable insights into the stress and overwhelm that many doctors experience in their day to day working lives, so I developed the niche of coaching doctors. However, I was aware the coaching approach differs from a medical consultation. Instead of prescriptive suggestions, a coach enables the client to find their best solution. I did this by asking them to think of options for change, even if these seemed impossible to achieve. Then I asked them about these, one by one, 'What's stopping you from doing this?' They realised they could try something they hadn't considered previously, and I encouraged them to do so.

I would ask my clients to prepare for their calls and let me know how they want to use the time. After the call, they thought about what we discussed and then took the action they promised.

Coaching doctors is a valuable niche to specialise in, especially if you come from a healthcare or medical background or have worked closely with members of the medical profession.

I believe that coaching can be very useful for doctors if you engage them with the process. However, since most doctors are highly intelligent, motivated and self-sufficient people, they may find it difficult to talk about challenges, as they see this as a sign of weakness.
If you persuade them that coaching can be useful, then they find it so.

Too often, **doctors find medicine consumes their days**. Just like a hungry monster which is never satisfied, there are always more things to do. As a result, I've noticed that many doctors are so overwhelmed by work that they have no time for anything or anyone else.

Doctors may contact a coach because they want to be less stressed about their career, getting on further in the profession, or because of pressures in their personal relationships.

However, in my experience, the most common issues that doctors wanted to discuss with me were:

Wanting more balance in their lives. Coaching around work-life balance includes discussing time management and self-care and the meaning of success. As a coach, I encouraged my doctor clients to recognise how vital it is to have a life outside of medicine. They don't fully understand the concept that there is more to life than medicine because there is so much pressure to pass exams to climb their perceived ladder of success.

A doctor's life is very stressful. An internet search for stress, burnout and doctors will bring up hundreds of articles about this common experience amongst doctors. Working as a doctor is not only challenging and busy but also interesting, so most doctors are passionate about medicine. Sometimes both they and others may wonder how they keep going with so much to do and so little time to do it. The work-load can overwhelm and there seems to be no way to lessen it.

However, there are ways that doctors can lead a fuller life so that medicine is fulfilling, yet combine this with a satisfying life outside of medicine. With coaching, they can discover ways to have more time for family and friends, their partner, their community, and for nurturing themselves body-mind-and-spirit and having fun.

During coaching, a doctor decided not to take her work diary home with her. This simple change enabled her to form a new boundary between work and leisure time, and she found she had renewed energy to enjoy her home life much more.

Another doctor left his briefcase at work and, as a result, enjoyed playing the piano once again.

Deciding about their next step. There is a lot of pressure on doctors to conform to perceived models of professional success. Doctors feel confused about the next stage in their career progression or the next stage in their life. They find it strange when told their goals can change depending on their life-stage. Unfortunately, even those doctors who make a positive decision for a different sort of lifestyle may find obstacles in their way.

A couple, both of whom are doctors, cannot find employment in the same town, so they have to live apart most of the time, have added expenses of renting extra accommodation.

Another young medical couple wants to start a family, but she could not continue her training on a part-time basis.

Since many doctors are unhappy about the state of their work-life balance, it's useful for a coach to guide and motivate them to find solutions which work for them.

There are ways to coach doctors to improve their work-life balance:

Establishing new boundaries. Doctors need to be clear about what they will or won't do. If they don't know this, then people they work with won't be clear either. Colleagues make unreasonable demands of them and their time. Doctors need to tell people when they cannot take on any more tasks. You could coach them to recognise which boundaries can change. For example, they might refuse to accept extra booking for a fully booked clinic but not be able to change the time the clinic is open.

Getting help and support from others. There is a culture amongst doctors to deal with everything themselves with no emotional support. Doctors may be very reluctant to ask for help from their colleagues or others because they perceive this as a sign of weakness. However, if they are overwhelmed with too much to do, then getting support and delegating more will mean they can improve their work-life balance. They must learn to explain precisely what they want the other person to do rather than saying "I need some help".

As a coach to doctors, you can encourage them to do this by pointing out that they have come forward to seek support from you. and so it will be a similar process to get further support from others. You could let them practice what they would say to the person they will delegate something to.

Having something to look forward to. If doctors are trying to leave work at a reasonable time and yet have nothing they want to do when they get home, then they are less likely to do this. Knowing that they have something to look forward to will be a powerful motivator.

You can coach them to plan what they want to do after work and be ready for it, for example, having their swimming things in the car with them so they can go swimming on the way home.

A medical client put her jogging shoes in her car in order to have a run before getting home.

Eating meals regularly. It's vital for doctors, as for everyone, to eat regularly and not go all day with no food or refreshment. They know how important it is but may need encouragement to eat healthy food and take a break during the day to eat it, from the coach.

Taking regular exercise. Exercise, like food, is extremely important. If they can't get out of the hospital during the day, then they must use any opportunity to walk from one end of hospital to the other.

A doctor client discovered that by walking with her children to school each day instead of taking them in the car, she not only had more energy to do her work but lost weight and felt fitter too.

16. Can coaching help doctors?

Coaching encourages doctors to bring more fun and laughter into their lives. It helps them realise this is vital for their health and well-being.

One way coaching motivates doctor clients is to encourage them to be more creative. Unfortunately, medical life suppresses creativity because much of the work is about following procedures in a prescribed way.

A coach can ask if the doctor has ever followed any creative pursuit, such as drawing, painting, photography, writing, singing, or music. The coach may suggest spending time each week doing whatever creative pastime they loved. This enables them to connect with their creative side again.

Some of my medical clients found a positive re-connection with: playing the piano, singing in a choir, gardening, photography, sculpture, painting, creative writing and woodwork.

When coaching doctors, help them change their mindset about what is or isn't possible and enable them to have less stressful lives. Encourage them to define what they want instead of the negativity they find themselves in. Once they know what they want rather than what they don't want, they find they can achieve more easily, through coaching.

If they say 'I hate getting home so late, I feel too exhausted to do anything else in the evening except eat and sleep,' they could change this to, 'I plan to arrive home an hour earlier so that I spend time with my children before they go to bed, or go for a swim or play tennis....' or whatever they would like if only they weren't so exhausted.

You can help doctors re-frame their statements about their beliefs into positive, solution-orientated statements. This moves them from concentrating on what they don't want to what they want. You encourage them to set goals for themselves which should, like all goals, be specific, measurable so they'll know when they've achieved them, as well as realistic and achievable within a stated time span.

Since it's important that doctors don't neglect their family and friends and spend all their time at work or thinking about their patients and other work-related issues, you can, with coaching, encourage your doctor clients to be more creative and think of new solutions to their challenges.

Ask the doctor 'What alternatives might there be to this situation?' Tell them to note the possibilities coming into their head and jot them down, however bizarre they seem to be, without judgement or editing. Then listen to them as they adapt their most strange ideas into practical solutions.

Challenging questions to ask your doctor clients might be:

If you had more time, what would you do with it?
How would you feel if you had time each week to do things you don't do now?
How could you better balance family life with work?

Here are some of the most important things doctors could do to make sure they don't neglect their family even though they may have a very busy job and work long hours and they find it difficult to "switch off" at the end of a busy day because they're constantly worrying whether they have done the right thing for their patients.

A coach encourages them to:

Spend quality time with their family every day, or some dedicated time every week. Even if all they do is to play with and read stories to their children for an hour every evening, they balance their work and other demands.

Make definite plans for when their family time will be. It really helps if they write this in their diary and treat it as important as any other appointment that they may have. If they have a very busy job, then it's easy to forget how important it is to spend time away from work enjoying being with family and friends.

Stop taking work home. It can become an automatic habit to bundle papers into a briefcase and say to themselves they will finish the work at home during the evening. It's better to plan their day, so they do as much as possible while they're at work. They must be realistic that there will always be jobs they can't finish in one day, and these can usually wait to be completed the following day.

Take regular holidays with their family. Some doctors find it difficult to balance family life and work. They only go away when there is a work-related function to attend and then expect members of the family to come along too. Instead, encourage them to plan a holiday in a location which has nothing to do with work. Decide what sort of activities they'll involve themselves in so they are fully occupied and can experience days away from both the work environment itself and worrying about work.

17. What does a coach do for doctors?

You may not have got around to coaching doctors because of being unclear about what to do when working with doctors.

A coach offers doctors:

Listening without judgment, so if a doctor is reluctant to talk because of expected recrimination about what they are talking about, then it is useful that you aren't judging them.

They can **brainstorm workable solutions** to their dilemma or problem when they talk to you and by so doing will realise the most appropriate way forward to make progress.

Questions to enable them to think more deeply. When they want to decide between different options, it is useful to be challenged by questions. These will enable them to think about ways to proceed that they may not have considered before.

Discovering ways to move forward. Having someone 'on their side' is very motivating and gets them to take actions they may have been procrastinating about.

Encouragement and help to get things done. If they feel stuck at a practical level, having someone who has 'been there, done that' is useful to give some pointers which can take them to their next step.

A chance to talk in confidence. Just knowing doctors can talk without what they say going further is very useful, because the coach supports their agenda and is not involved directly in their life.

Insight into some of their own experience. Despite sharing, it can be helpful for them to hear how someone else coped with something similar. If the coach has the same profession, they may want to learn from what happened. However, they realise that the way each person deals with a particular circumstance may depend on their own perception and personality. Just knowing that there might be some connection between their life and yours can be helpful.

The importance of self-care. When doctors care for themselves, they will be in a better state to care for others more effectively. People who work in the caring professions, such as doctors, may forget how important it is to look after themselves. They may be perfectionists and believe that they must always put the care of others before caring for themselves. How many hours they work, and however much they do, there must come a point at which they stop. This may be because they've finished all the tasks that need to be done, or they are so exhausted that they cannot do even one more thing. Unfortunately, what stops some doctors in their tracks is finding they have developed an illness and need to take some time away from work.

Only then do they realise they are not indispensable and although it is important to work efficiently as a doctor, it is also important to have time away from medicine too.

Doctors who don't look after themselves find the quality of their work deteriorates. They take longer to do routine tasks and become more likely to make mistakes and may become a liability. Doctors who don't look after themselves are more likely to prescribe the wrong treatment or the wrong dose, with subsequent serious effects both for the patient and the doctor themself. They may also drink excessive alcohol or self-medicate instead of seeking the help and support they need.

The responsibility of working as a doctor is huge and making a mistake might be disastrous. However, with the pressures put on doctors, there may be a tendency to work hard and forget how important it is to spend time away from work. Whether they worry about how they dealt with the last patient, or prepare for a presentation for their colleagues, or try to keep up to date with medical journal reading, life is stressful for doctors.

18. Doctors' Challenges

The biggest challenges for doctors that are helped with coaching are:

Goal setting: I've found that doctors, in common with many other clients need coaching around developing their long-term vision about their life and then chunking it down to achievable goals and from them into smaller steps, making the step from concentrating on what they don't want to what they want.

Work life balance: It's important to understand what a challenge this is for doctors. The medical profession is all-consuming. However, when you encourage your doctor clients to connect with what they used to enjoy but believe they no longer have time for, they will have more balanced lives.

Managing time: an essential skill for busy professionals such as doctors to develop for making space for a more balanced life.

 Self-care: doctors know all about this but may find it a challenge to apply to themselves: coaching can enable them to do so when you help them identify ways, they can improve their own health and well-being make a commitment to themselves to improve this.

Environment and behaviour: coaching helps doctors improve their environment. For example, flowers brighten a dull office; a cheery good morning changes their mood.

Capability: doctors need new skills. Coaching can identify these and motivate them. I've coached doctors to be more assertive.

Beliefs and Values: your doctor client may understand with coaching that some powerful beliefs are just that, rather than fixed facts and that they can change.

Identity: with coaching doctors realise **they are more than their profession** and how important it is to notice more of themselves.

Purpose: I've found that many doctors have a great sense of purpose. They need to come to terms with what they can do in order to keep a sense of proportion. Some discover a reason they are here and by doing this, a coach motivates them to achieve what they want, rather than the expected medical-based life purpose.

Communication skills: doctors spend a lot of time talking to patients. Some doctors have challenges in communicating with colleagues. Coaching around confidence, assertiveness and rapport is important. They need to communicate more effectively.

Stress management: since many doctors find their professional life is very stressful, they benefit from techniques to reduce or get rid of stress such as taking time out for relaxation and other pursuits away from medicine, and taking a minute or two between patients to breathe out any stress.

Creativity: a doctor may experience pressure to follow rigid procedures. Coaching enables them to connect with their creativity, whether this is through writing, painting or playing music.

Doctors believe they are indispensable: but one day, they may not work. If so, they must take time to recover fully. Doctors are bad at taking time away from work to recover. They feel guilty about letting their patients down and even more; they realise their colleagues have to do much more work to cover for their absence until they return. They know that even with good locum cover, there will be a considerable number of their patients who would rather wait to see their doctor when he or she returns.

All these factors can cause a doctor not taking enough time to recover from their illness and so they may return and are less able to cope with the workload, take more time to do simple tasks and cannot work as efficiently or even as competently as before.

When doctors take care of themselves and their own needs, they cope effortlessly with their patients.

They need a coach to support them unconditionally and not wait until they become so exhausted that they become burnt out and have to take early retirement on health grounds.

19. Coaching, one to one or in a group?

Coaching enables doctors to improve their lifestyle. In some situations, being part of a group is commonplace for doctors, especially when discussing clinical decisions.

A group format can be of benefit when used for personal development. There are small peer support groups set up for groups of doctors to meet regularly so the members can give and receive support. Coaches could facilitate groups too, perhaps combined with a course encompassing aspects of personal development. Coaches are often more familiar with working with people on the telephone or on the internet. Small group coaching can be useful for doctors. However, they may resist joining a group because they don't want to appear to need help.

You could encourage them that being part of a supportive group is for them if they want to:

- *Make changes*
- *Have more time*
- *Stop feeling stressed*
- *Become fitter*
- *Feel happier*
- *Recognise they have choices*
- *Enjoy the synergy and support of a group.*

A coach running a group for doctors offers support, encouragement and motivation. However, in my experience, there is a built-in resistance amongst doctors about admitting vulnerability about not being able to cope with something, so there are challenges for a coach wanting to set up such a group.

As well as groups meeting on the telephone or online, there are other ways to offer support, such as forums aimed at doctors or email groups. These would all give some amount of anonymity and solve the problem of travelling to a place to meet. In the UK, there are some groups already set up for this purpose.

You could setup a support group for doctors using the usual marketing channels: such as article marketing sending doctors to your website to sign up for a free report or recording to introduce them to your work. You could build a list of interested doctors. What you decide to charge for any support would depend on the 'going rate' in your area, as well as the perceived value of what you are offering.

Whether coaching is one to one or as a small group, it benefits doctors because:

It involves gaining clarity. They will explain to the coach details of their situation and the challenges they face. If they have a coach with whom they feel comfortable, they talk about what's happening, and talking and considering answers to the coaches' questions will help them understand themselves better and find their own solution.

Coaching enables them to find their own solution.
The coach asks challenging questions and helps them think again about their long-held beliefs or assumptions in relation to what is possible. Since it is not prescriptive doctors can discover within themselves options for progress, they may not have thought of previously.

The coach encourages them.
Coaching motivates them to do what they want to do and discover for themselves the right way forward without the judgmental attitude that friends or family may bring when they try to find a solution with them.

Coaching is forward looking.
It is effective quickly, so doctors have the energy and motivation to change things and make a difference within a few sessions.

Coaching can be on the telephone. The coach can concentrate on what they say rather than making quick judgements that are commonplace when clients are face to face. A coach familiar with working on the telephone can detect shifts in meaning and emotion from the tone of voice, the answers given, and the pauses before they answer a question.

20. Doctors know about coaching

Doctors are likely to hear about coaching in the press or on television and may wonder what it is and if it might be useful, but something has held them back from exploring the option of hiring a coach. Perhaps they thought it was a bit 'wishy-washy' or too 'touchy-feely'.

They may have wondered if other doctors have benefited from coaching and since they've heard it's about finding their own solutions, believe that they should be able to sort things out for themselves without involving a coach, especially someone who doesn't know them and who they might never meet except on the telephone.

Here are some questions you could ask potential doctor clients to help them decide if coaching would be useful.

Do they really want a different sort of life? A doctor's life can be intense and can engulf them so they neglect other important parts of their life. However, the thought of changing it may be scary and they would rather stick with what they are familiar with, even if they aren't happy with it.

Are they prepared to talk about what isn't working for them but to picture the sort of life they would really like and the options they have for living that way?

Unless they look to their future and discuss the options and possibilities, it will be difficult to make the changes they want.

Do they realise that success can encompass all aspects of their life, not only their medical work? Many doctors define success in relation to their work and so strive to get to the top of their specialty and yet have an unfulfilling personal life.

Would they be able to see things from a new perspective? If they continue doing everything in exactly the same way, then nothing changes. Even if they think the system has to change, there are things they can do to make this happen. This may mean expressing their concerns about the routines, or telling others how they are going to be doing something from now onwards.

Can they understand it is important to look at their whole life, not only at the part who is the doctor? Their whole life involves their partner, friends and family and their community. It also includes those parts of they not involved in medicine, their hobbies and outside interests, the way they look after their own health and well-being too.

21. 'Culture' of the medical profession

Is it true that doctors are strong enough to deal with whatever they see or hear? As human beings, doctors, as much as anyone, are affected by some patients more than others. There will be some about whom they feel particularly upset or concerned. Sigmund Freud called this 'transference.' It happens when something about the patient connects with something or someone in their own lives. They may not be aware of the connection but know that some patients seem very interesting or raise particular concerns for them while others seem to bore and they are not very interested in what has been happening to them.

Unlike counsellors who are supported by regular supervision from someone to help them sort out what issues are the client's and what are their own, doctors have to deal with all of this themselves with little support. Some doctors are recognising the value of coaching to fulfil this function too.

When doctors experience the power of support and encouragement rather than demands and intimidation, they will be more able to learn to use coaching skills with their patients rather than reaching for the prescription pad or becoming exasperated.

When someone listens to their concerns and acknowledges them as legitimate, they will become a better listener to their patients and hear more of their underlying issues and be able to empower them, too. They will convey to them they can make a difference to their own lives when they take responsibility for it. Every minor change they, as individuals, make will eventually help to change the system for all doctors and health professionals.

22. Improving work-life balance?

When coaching doctors about improving their work-life balance, you will also coach them about managing their time more effectively, one of the most common challenges that many doctors face. When they aren't time-aware, the medical work seems to be endless and takes priority over the rest of their life.

This means that their work-life balance suffers. They felt overwhelmed, frustrated, didn't sleep well, and become less efficient. This affects their life outside of work too. Not only does it affect their friends and family but also their relationship with their partner. Most crucial of all is on their own health and well-being because when they cannot manage their time effectively, their personal physical and emotional health can suffer too.

Busy doctors overwhelmed with how much they have to do each day could be encouraged to manage their time more effectively so they have the time to be with family and friends, and do those things they enjoy but haven't had the time or energy for many years.

Most doctors are overworked and don't have enough time to do things they used to enjoy outside of work. Their partner, family and friends complain they are always working and they hardly ever see them. Even when they join in social activities, they are not good company as they are exhausted and may fall asleep during a social occasion.

If they leave work late each day and also take work home, remind them they are not superhuman and just like every other human being, need some time away from work to enjoy sport and hobbies and being with partner, friends and family and also time for themselves.

This feeling of being overworked and constantly tired seems to have become part of medical life: a choice of either forget the rest of life or leave medicine. Some deal with the stress by drinking or eating too much. Some decide to pack it all in and leave the profession. However, there are alternatives. They can define boundaries of what they will do, when they will stop, and clarify what they can achieve each day. Coaching enables them to do this.

When you are coaching doctors about time management, encourage them to consider:
Being clear about what has to be done. If they are confident about which clinics, ward rounds, visits, and patients have to be attended to or dealt with each day. By clarifying exactly what they have to do each day, they will work more systematically and find they have time and energy left for out of work activities.

Becoming more efficient. If you encourage doctors to plan so that they know what has to be done, within the constraints of working as a doctor, then they will get more done each day by coordinating their different activities so they don't have to go over the same things several times. They may need to be encouraged to delegate more, work quickly and ask for help when necessary, since, in my experience, doctors like to do things themselves. However, when they agree to do this, they will think more clearly about the patient in front of them instead of worrying about what they did earlier with other patients or what still needs to be done that day.

Keeping the end in mind. We should urge doctors to avoid distractions from other non-urgent, non-important things by keeping focussed on their goals for the day and completing them, one step at a time. If they are doing a clinic, for example, they could clarify that they do not want to be interrupted, except with extreme emergency.

Explaining that variety is the spice of life. When doctors get overwhelmed, they find that doing different tasks enables them to keep on top of several things. For example, after seeing a few patients, they could do some administrative tasks before going back to seeing more patients. This keeps them moving on with what has to be done and ensures that they are not having to do an enormous task.

Reminding doctors to celebrate their achievements day by day and their progress towards their goals. Doctors get frustrated if they feel they are not getting much done. They are probably doing more than they thought they were. If they make a list and tick the items as they do them, they will recognise their progress and feel a great sense of achievement too. It might be useful to suggest they keep a file of 'thank-you' letters too so they can read these on days when they feel particularly fed up and overwhelmed.

Being more time aware. When they are talking to patients about their symptoms and finding out their medical history, it's easy to lose track of the time. To prevent this, doctor could train themselves to be more aware of how long the consultation and examination takes and keep a prominently displayed clock to learn how to gain the information they need more quickly, while allowing the patient to tell what they want.

Starting the working day earlier. Instead of arriving at the same time as the first patient, it can be very useful to start their day earlier. By arriving up to an hour before their first appointment, doctors can catch up with correspondence, emails or other administrative tasks or use the time to talk to colleagues about concerns or patients they wish to discuss with them. Doing this enables them to start the day's work, knowing they have already sorted out other issues.

Taking a break during the day. Deciding to take regular breaks may seem to be an oxymoron when there is so much to do. However, taking some time off, even a half an hour, in the middle of the day will give the chance to re-charge their batteries and thus be more efficient during the rest of the day.

Reviewing their working practice. If they stop doing what doesn't have to be done by them or anyone else, delegate more by training someone else who could take on some of their routine tasks, and do what only they can do, more quickly by devising efficient systems.

Looking forward to something unrelated to work. Knowing that they look forward to doing what they enjoy away from medical work is an effective incentive to discovering ways to manage their time and thus their lives more effectively.

Manage their time and work-life balance better by:

- keep to designated time when seeing patients
- take a break for lunch
- stop taking work home
- meet some friends
- have a laugh
- do not take life seriously
- have a regular holiday
- take a few moments every day to relax

Life changes for the better and the doctors have more energy, feel happier, get through the workload more quickly and enjoy life when they change.

23. Telephone coaching

Coaching motivates people to change and achieve their goals. *I trained to become a coach through conference calls over a couple of years. Since I was comfortable using the telephone for coaching, I never met my clients face to face.*

Here are the advantages of coaching doctors on the telephone or online.

Is it really as simple as it sounds?
What about body language and building rapport?
How do you know how they are feeling, or their mood?
You tune into the tone of their voice, the words they use, the silences, their speed of talking so you can sense whether they are smiling or crying, whether what they are telling you is painful or a cause for celebration.
You do this within a coaching relationship. When you can't see body language, you become much more sensitive to other clues. You already do this when you use the telephone to talk to friends, family and colleagues.

What advantages might there be?
The coaching relationship is based on suitability rather than geography. Doctors can be anywhere in the country or the world.

Why isn't the telephone used more widely?

Doctors may assume, wrongly, that coaching must take place face to face. They believe that coaching is like a medical consultation. Because doctor-patient consultations happen face to face, (though increasingly nowadays on the telephone too), some assume that coaching must be the same. They are reluctant to consider alternatives. Encourage them to try something different. There has to be a serious consideration of more widespread use of the telephone.

I coached all my doctor clients on the telephone. They would ask me 'Where are you based?' My answer was: 'Wherever you are, I am a long way from there.' Some who were cynical at first agreed it worked well. Coaching is more manageable using the telephone or connecting on-line.

Convenience: The more widespread use of the telephone or internet as a means of communication is the way forward. It makes coaching more accessible for those who want to give or receive coaching.

No geographical restriction: You can have a good coaching relationship with your client wherever they live or work. If you are on the opposite sides of the world, you can enable positive change.

Efficient use of time and energy: Face-to-face meetings mean some travel, even if within the same area. Use of the telephone avoids this.

Less time and money spent on travel: This is important with high cost of fuel or train fares. You can spend the designated time talking instead of time and stress getting to a meeting place.

Avoids physical stereotyping: You make judgments within 30 seconds of seeing them. Using the telephone prevents this. Coaching relationships can fail if the meeting place is distracting, or you don't like the look of each other.

Less distraction: You can concentrate on the interaction between you both and not be side-tracked by surroundings. This means that you experience a greater focus on what they say.

Boundaries are clear: You start and finish the session within the designated time. Arranging a telephone or on-line meeting is straightforward and time saving. It's simple to define the meeting length and to be more time-aware. For some, it may be easier for a more open discussion, too. Both of you can make notes more easily: clients say they take copious notes. This might be off-putting if you were meeting in person. There can be more confidentiality too because no-one sees you meeting.

Sessions can be one to one or in groups. During a well-organised conference call, there is a valuable exchange of ideas. If well facilitated, a group that meets on the telephone or on-line can give and receive support from others.

Note-taking is easy: clients say they take copious notes. This might be off-putting if you were meeting in person.

You already have the skills to use the telephone or on-line methods for coaching and make it manageable.

What reasons are there for reluctance by some doctors to be coached on the telephone?
How does talking on the telephone differ from face-to-face consultations?

A practical challenge you may have with medical coaching might be that of finding someone suitable to work with in your geographical area. Perhaps you find it stressful in relation to the time to meet. This factor alone may make regular meetings less likely.

Do you wonder if some of your coaching/mentoring relationships fail because you find the meeting place distracting, or even that you don't like the look of the person with whom you've been paired?

Could you resolve these challenges simply?
Yes, by meeting on the telephone.
Is it really as simple as it sounds?

What about body language and building rapport?
You already do this when you use the telephone to talk to friends, family and colleagues. When you use the telephone or Internet extensively, a coach and a client can be anywhere in the world.

Sessions can be one to one or in groups. During a well-organised conference call, there is a valuable exchange of ideas. If well facilitated, a group that meets on the telephone or on-line can give and receive support from others.

What advantages might there be?
The partnership based on suitability rather than on geography. Doctors can be anywhere in the country or the world.

Arranging a telephone or on-line meeting is straightforward and time saving. It's simple to define the meeting length and to be more time-aware. For some, it may be easier for a more open discussion, too.
For both, it's less obtrusive to take notes while on the telephone. There can be more confidentiality too because neither of you can see the other one.

The case for telephone or on-line coaching: The more widespread use of the telephone or internet as a means of communication for medical coaching is the way forward to making this support more accessible if you want to either give or receive coaching.

How do you know how they are feeling, or their mood? You can tune into the tone of their voice, the words they use, the silences, their speed of talking so that you can sense whether they are smiling or crying, whether what they are telling you is painful or a cause for celebration. Similarly, you can do this within a coaching/mentoring relationship. When you can't see body language, you become much more sensitive to other clues.

Do you wonder about how effective telephone coaching might be?
Don't assume it won't work. Be prepared to try something differently that may be useful.

Emotion. We can recognise emotion on the telephone. Have you ever had a phone call from a friend to say they have won a prize or passed their exam or that someone has just died? You know their emotional state without seeing their face. Silences can be important. Allow them to happen.

Rapport. This might be more difficult to establish, but not necessarily. Think about telephone conversations you have with friends and colleagues and how quickly you create a connection with them.

Belief. You may think that you can't coach as effectively on the telephone if you believe it isn't as good as face to face. This is a limiting belief. Think about how much you use the telephone in other situations (for example, talking to friends, family, and colleagues). You probably already have excellent telephone communication skills.

Body language. Since you can't see each other, rely on other clues. When using the telephone, your listening skills improve and you have a sense of the other person from the tone and volume of voice. The words not used may be as important as what they say.

Skills. It's important that you let go of finding solutions and that the doctor trusts that they can find their own answers. The telephone allows freedom for expression of thoughts and ideas.

Confidentiality. Doctors may worry about someone overhearing the conversation. For telephone coaching, as with face to face, choose somewhere private. Using the telephone allows greater privacy for the coaching session.

Coaching: the way forward. We already used the telephone for schemes that offer other support to doctors, such as The Doctors Support Line and the BMA counselling service.

We accept mentoring and coaching methods, enabling doctors to cope with the stresses of medical life. To be even more effective, there has to be a serious consideration of more widespread use of the telephone or on-line sessions.

PART FOUR - MY STORY

24. My story

I started coaching in 2000. Previously a medical practitioner and counsellor living and working in inner city Birmingham, I retired from medicine in 1997 to live another sort of life. Working as a doctor for over thirty years with a husband and three children had kept me enjoyably busy, but I wanted to do something different and creative.

I discovered coaching via Louise Hay's books and workshops and plenty of personal development. My epiphany was reading about coaching in a woman's magazine in July 1999, following which I trained and graduated with Coach University. I returned to my medical roots as 'the doctors coach' and specialised in coaching doctors who contact her from wherever they live. I coached by telephone or by email, so it didn't matter where the clients were. I had articles published in the British Medical journal each month and was author of the first coaching book for doctors.

Life after medicine?
I finally took the plunge in 1997 and wrote my letter of resignation. At fifty-four, I had enough of busy clinics, demanding and aggressive patients, increasing paperwork, decreasing funding and low morale of colleagues. Too many rules and regulations, too many forms to fill in and too much talk of data and being on target.

I wanted desperately to be more creative and do things I never had time for when I was busy with the demands of a family and work. I loved painting, not bowls of fruit or landscapes but letting the brush go where it wants to go -and dreamed of having time to cover enormous canvases with brightly coloured paints. I also wrote a novel: an entirely new experience for me and wanted to develop my writing skills further.

However, not everyone saw things my way; my colleagues and my family did their best to dissuade me. They told me I was too young to retire, that I was good at my job, that the patients would ask for me, and that I would miss them and that I would hanker after the work.

'What are you going to do with yourself, won't you be bored?' they asked.

I put the same question to myself and wrote every day in my journal to help find the answers. I knew what I wanted, but no-one encouraged me. (I wish I had a coach, but I'd never heard of coaching then and anyway I was a doctor I could deal with anything myself!)

Looking back, all that was water under the bridge once I was coaching doctors as clients. I loved my new life too much to go back to the old one! I found a way of looking at problems and helping people find their own solutions. As a doctor I was 'the expert' but as a coach the client is the ultimate authority for their life.

When I qualified back in 1967, there was a very paternalistic attitude toward the patient/doctor relationship. Interactions with patients comprised 'Here is my problem, what can you do about it?' As the doctor, I used my skill and experience to decide the source of the problem. 'Here is a prescription. Take these' or ' you need to see a specialist.'

As a coach, I used a fresh approach. I brought my life experiences and my training to coaching. I helped clients find their own answers to their difficulties. For example, I helped them find time to do what they wanted to do, by eliminating time wasters and delegating tasks to others and dropping some 'to do's' completely. The clients realised what they dreamt of was within their grasp if they worked out what first steps to take. I shared experiences, if relevant, but no longer assumed my way is the only way. I've become more tolerant. I was the catalyst which enabled my clients to change their lives.

For myself, I found time to do things I was too busy to do before. I wrote, painted, travelled and read books. I designed and set up my web-site. I trekked across glaciers in Alaska and sand dunes in Namibia, in aid of charities.

I benefited from several coaches over the years who motivated and challenged me. It was wonderful to have someone who encouraged me to do what I wanted. We met on the telephone for a focussed coaching discussion three times a month. This regular contact with discussion, goal setting and reporting back was enormously motivating.

I've been thinking about the changes in the NHS and the low morale and frustration of many doctors. The word 'doctor' links to the word 'stressed.' I read about harassed consultants and GPs buckling under the strain of the NHS and wonder if one day coaching would become more widely used and accepted amongst doctors. Coaching helped me realise that looking after my physical and emotional needs is vital. Balance in all areas of life is paramount. I've learned to say no more often and to set clearer boundaries, both physical and emotional. I get rid of things that drain me and increase what gives me energy. There is life after medicine!

When I qualified, the patient asked what I would about it?' As a doctor, they expected me to know the diagnosis, how to investigate and the treatment.

As a coach, I learned to use a fresh approach to encourage my client to find their own answers. This enabled them to discover for themselves, with my support, how to do what they wanted. They could eliminate time-wasting, delegate tasks, be more efficient and drop some 'to-dos' completely and enjoy a more balanced life. They realised that what they dreamt of doing was within their grasp.

I shared my own experiences, if relevant, but no longer assumed that my way is the only way because instead I was a catalyst for people to change their lives.

For those wanting to leave medicine, for whatever reason, I followed their agenda, not mine, about what was missing during their working years and what they dreamt of doing.

I avoided telling someone that what he or she dreamt of was possible or impossible. I asked challenging questions so they could discover for themselves their way forward.

25. How I found doctors to coach

My experience as a doctor gave me special insights about life as a doctor, so I concentrated on coaching doctors. However, I had to discover ways to find doctors who would benefit from the coaching I offered.

How did my clients find me?
I wrote a brief article, 'Is there life after medicine?' hoping that they would publish it in 'Personal View' in the BMJ, but the panel rejected it, (maybe because the message in the article was 'yes there is!'). However, Rhona MacDonald contacted me. She was the editor of Career Focus (part of the BMJ). She encouraged me to write a series of articles about coaching and how it enabled doctors to have a life.

Every month, for several years, I was fortunate to be asked to write regular articles about personal development for doctors, such as how doctors could have more time and better work-life balance; how they could look after themselves; ways to achieve their goals.

They published these each month in the British Medical Journal. These included my website and email address at the end of each article. As a result, doctors contacted me and I ran workshops for doctors with coaching themes such as work life balance and time management. The articles grew into books about personal development for doctors.

I listened to doctor's challenges and enable them to find solutions. I used my medical and life experiences as I developed the niche of coaching doctors.

My way is not your way. You already know how to proceed and find the clients in your way of coaching. If you are ready to pursue coaching doctors as a worthwhile niche, then work with a coach to discover how that works for you. Doctors are ready and waiting.

If you are a coach, make sure you work with a mentor or coach yourself because it's useful to experience for yourself the benefit that mentoring or coaching brings.

Everyone benefits, most of all, yourself. You'll discover at first-hand how beneficial it is to have someone to offload and bounce ideas onto and listen to you talk about the things which seem insoluble in your life.

I've learned is that life is an ongoing process of change, finding solutions along the way, both for you and your clients, whether continuing to work as doctors, or deciding to leave medicine.

Don't miss out!

Visit the website below and you can sign up to receive emails whenever Susan Kersley publishes a new book. There's no charge and no obligation.

https://books2read.com/r/B-A-EFNC-MVIL

Connecting independent readers to independent writers.

Did you love Lifestyle Coaching for Doctors?
Then you should read **Prescription for Change** by Susan Kersley!

This book is a catalyst for doctors to have the life they want. It promotes a healthy work life balance and is a practical easy to read guide with useful tips and advice for doctors to be less stressed and enjoy life more. Written by Susan Kersley, a retired doctor who worked in the N.H.S for thirty years. This book is for doctors who wonder if they can continue working in Medicine and want to discover ways to make their lives happier and more balanced.

Also by Susan Kersley

A Novel
Pills and Pillboxes
Connection Deception

Books about Weight Management
Change Your Mind, Change Your Weight
Mind Over Weight
Weight Loss Success

Books for Doctors
ABC of Change for Doctors
Simple Ways to Meet the Challenges of Working as a Doctor
Critical Mistakes Nearly Every Doctor Makes
Life After Medicine
More than 80 ways for a Busy Doctor to have more time
Prescription for Time
Prescription for Change
Work-Life Balance for Doctors
Strategies for Doctors to Connect and Change
Lifestyle Coaching for Doctors

Retirement Books
Get Ready for Retirement
Life After Work
Retirement: Back to Basics

Self-help Books
How to Have a Balanced Life
15 Ways to Change Your Life
69 Easy Ways to Change Your life
Coping With New Year Resolutions
More Time for You Now

About the Author

Susan Kersley has written personal development and self-help books for doctors and others, and books about retirement and novels. She was a doctor for thirty years and then left Medicine to be a Life Coach.

Now retired, she is updating her books and writing more.

Please visit her website https://susankersley.co.uk

If you enjoyed this book, please take a moment to leave a review. Reviews are so important for independent authors.

Printed in Great Britain
by Amazon

18074745R00058